In this latest collection, Ro. _____ _____ deitly revisits themes common in his preceding work: grief, death, anger, injustice, the past. Also here, though, is something new: a profound longing for a world from which—through injury, illness, and age— he has become increasingly exiled. Almost entirely confined for the past six years to a small studio apartment, the room and the bit of space immediately outside his windows serve as the backdrop for many of the poems in this book. His loneliness, frustration, and dread are as keenly expressed as felt.

Despite all this, it's not relentlessly grim. This tapestry of poems is threaded with Smith's signature black humor. Lighter moments of whimsy, and poems about his beloved cat, sparkle brilliantly amid the darkness to create a balanced collection.

Most significantly, Smith still holds within himself an inextinguishable appreciation of the everyday miracles that surround us even in the smallest of domains. Spiderwebs receive the same attention as the stars, and something as simple as wind moving through trees is beautifully exalted:

> "The leaves beneath the streetlight,
> stirring in a barely noticeable breeze,
> glow like soft green wings
> poised on the brink of flight.
>
> They are the only angels
> I will ever need."

Among myriad other natural aspects, it's fitting that birds in particular appear often in this book. They function as a sort of Greek chorus to the poet's life, but they are also capable of flight, and Smith's heart can—and does—occasionally soar with them.

—Janet Wildung, author of *The Archaeology of Negative Space*

THIS LATE
IN THE SEASON

THIS LATE
IN THE SEASON

Poems

ROBERT LAVETT SMITH

Full Court Press
Englewood Cliffs, New Jersey

First Edition

Copyright © 2024 by Robert Lavett Smith

Published in the United States of America
by Full Court Press, 601 Palisade Avenue,
Englewood Cliffs, NJ 07632
fullcourtpress.com

ISBN 978-1-953728-36-4
Library of Congress Control No. 2024914989

Editing and book design by Barry Sheinkopf

ACKNOWLEDGMENTS

Some of these poems first appeared in the online journal *The Hypertexts,* edited by Michael R. Burch.

"For A Black Unicorn" first appeared in the anthology *Remembering Audre Lorde,* published by the Moonstone Press and edited by Larry Robin.

I acknowledge both of these publications with deep gratitude.

FOR BILL KLINGELHOFFER

"There's nothing as scary as the future."
—*John Irving*

Table of Contents

PART ONE: THE GRACE OF OTHERS DANCING

PART TWO: YOU MAY BEGIN

PART THREE: EXTRAVAGANT BEAUTY EVERYWHERE

PART ONE

The Grace
of Others Dancing

THIS L...

WINTER

LIGHTNING

After reading Lynn Ungar

What blessing can I,
who have never believed
in a personal god,
offer a new year
that in my neighborhood at least
is already bitter cold
and gray with rain?

From somewhere beyond words
the darkness answers me:
no sacrament is needed
save for the grace of acceptance.

It all goes on.
Galaxies whirl like pinwheels
beyond the range
of even our most
far-sighted telescopes.

And before too many
more years have passed
it will go on without me,
though I hold in my mouth
like the sudden taste
of winter lightning
my wonder at the miracle
that I, or any of this,
was ever here at all.

WHAT RISES INSTEAD

At the very least,
I expect the rain to sweeten,
if only for an hour or two,
the air, which so close to the ocean
smells always of brine,
the restless winter wind,
and brown, exhausted fog.

But when it falls steadily
for many days on end,
what rises instead is the stench
of dead things in the soil,
a sort of half-hearted resurrection
keenly felt among the deepest roots
and in the dreamless realms of worms.

THUNDER

Yesterday morning,
safe and dry indoors,
I heard the hiss
of an insistent rain,
followed by the hollow
sound of thunder—
a rarity in this climate
at any time of year.
In the several decades
since I moved west,
it's a sound I've heard
maybe four times at most,
not counting of course
those sleepless nights
when I played a record
of a thunderstorm
from dusk until dawn,
that my unwanted vigil
might be at least
a bit less lonely.

THE UNASSAILABLE
SPLENDOR OF LIGHT

"Until flesh is glass."
                                    —*Joseph Fasano*

Little remains any longer
of the ordinary, unnoticed things
we handled throughout our marriage:
dropped goblets that shattered
into a thousand tiny, deadly shards,
neither splinters nor stars;
the hand-painted coffee mugs—
ugly—that we got as wedding gifts,
whose clumsy splashes of random color
bespoke a bored factory worker somewhere
with no artistic talent.

And nothing at all remains now
of your beloved body
consigned to a crematorium furnace,
or of your ashes given in turn
to a bitter wind one January dawn,
from a private plane
above the Golden Gate—
so quickly dispersed
that to all intents and purposes
they vanished into nothingness.

I like to think that as your body burned
your bones incandesced
like molten glass,
the earthly fragility of flesh
exchanged in an instant

for the unassailable splendor of light,
like the glassblower's liquid fire
endlessly reshaped
by a simple exhalation of breath.

A THANKSGIVING BLESSING

For the nonce, at least, while the steamy air
is fat with the promise of sage and cornbread,
and overfed fowl whose vestigial wings
never tested any wind are crisped brown
for the sacrifice, may we reclaim the reverence
of those first pilgrims for whom the unruly land
must have seemed a cruelly compelling Canaan.

IMAGINARY FRIEND

"Say a word,
Then listen to it fray..."
                    —*Charles Simic*

Even in the company of others,
I have often been lonely enough
to have learned to talk to myself,
my only dependable company.

I've always had a tendency
to speak loudly, fostered, I think,
by the realization, quite early on,
that no one was listening.

I suppose I raised my voice
in an unconscious effort
to combat the incessant
white noise of indifference.

This was more similar than
you might reasonably expect
to some children's reliance
upon an imaginary friend.

Having been unheard
for far too many years,
I gradually began to doubt
the very fact of my existence.

THAT WHICH IS COMING

"To that which is coming, I say,
Here, take what is yours."
                    —Jane Hirshfield

That which is coming
has been en route for years,
shuffling slowly through
the shifting seasons,
its footsteps like the calm
that settles at daybreak
after nights hurt by wind.

The new moon wants it
attired in black, its robes
sequined with faint stars,
but it wears more easily
the green of new leaves
comprised entirely of light.

All my life I have sensed
its inexorable approach,
and I'm surprised to find
that without my noticing
it has drawn quite near.

Dozens of songbirds
circle above its head
like a feathered halo,
embroidering the dawn
with a cacophony of song—
sparrows, warblers, and larks,
when I'd expected crows.

FOR ALL MY DEAD

New leaves cup silences
in brimming bowls of green light
on rare mornings without wind.
The air is a page already turning
before the ink of loss is dry.

DOROTHY GALE DREAMS IN COLOR

Thanksgiving night,
I watched the *Wizard of Oz*
through headphones on my laptop,
in a deliberate if solitary homage
to those Thanksgivings of my childhood
when, in the New York area, at least,
families always gathered
in the living room after dinner
to revisit the movie on TV
over cocoa and minced pie.
By the time I was in high school,
we finally had a color set,
so I experienced Dorothy's astonishment
as she stepped from the drab sepia
of the Dust Bowl
into the brilliant Technicolor
of the land over the rainbow.

If her adventure was indeed a dream,
then Dorothy Gale dreams in color,
just as I always have—
and waking to the near monochrome
of autumn in the Sunset District,
especially in these latter years
when the leaves whisper grimly
and the wind is steadily rising,
I too have sometimes wished
to be transported to a place
where troubles melt like lemon drops,
although the sky here
is cloudy, close, and cold
even on days without rain,

and I haven't seen a bluebird,
happy or otherwise,
in simply ages.

JANUARY MORNING

After a cold night, ice on the puddles,
breached by seeds from nearby trees,
is spiderwebbed like shattered glass.
If there are birds, I cannot hear them.
Nothing disturbs the solidity
of the unflinching metallic sky.

BARNSTORMING

"...something amazing, a boy falling out of the sky..."
—W. H. Auden, 1907–1973

Barnstorming was a big deal in the thirties.
By then the planes were slightly more robust
than the Blériot XI that turned heads
when it passed over town in 1912.

But wooden wings of resin-stiffened cloth
were nothing one would dare rely upon
should sudden thunderstorms rise in the east,
as happened in July of '34.

A wing walker—some hothead from Topeka—
must have lost either his footing or his nerve
when, shaken by an unexpected gust,
the Sopwith bucked and plunged him to his death.

Ralph Channing, whose forefather built the church,
newly ordained and just returned from Boston,
preached his first sermon to a bumper crop
of mourners in dark veils and patched black suits.

Avoiding the expected Christian themes,
Ralph built his homily on Icarus,
warning the congregation that the Lord
is best approached through charity and prayer.

"But who among us hasn't sometimes flown
too near the sun?" the greenhorn preacher asked.
The farmers in the pews, their skin burnt brown,
took up their hymnals, nodding in agreement.

WHAT THEY KNEW

"What they knew is worth a record, a few notes."
—*Mark Jarman*

In childhood, my parents knew
the poverty of the Depression,
the flat light of the lake plain,
the low skies in winter
gray and already fading
like a forgotten photograph.
The only color in their world
spilled through stained glass
on Sundays, like the touch
of a God in whom neither believed.
Near Buffalo, where Dad was raised,
the silence of his father's dairy farm
turned every day into a sort of sabbath,
though there was never really any rest.
Two hundred miles west, in Ohio,
Mom woke at night to the moans
of freights clattering through town,
past the mill and the water tower,
bound for somewhere else.

THE GRACE OF OTHERS DANCING

"The dark that loves is what we feel."
— *Annie Finch*

As I've grown older,
it has become necessary,
after decades of loss,
to labor at gratitude.

Unable to dance,
I have learned instead
to admire the grace
of others dancing.

I've grown to appreciate
the beauty of an old guitar,
although my clumsy fingers
can coax no music from its strings.

Every night at dusk,
I'm reminded the dark loves me,
as the seraphic crows
croak their broken hosannas.

So little light is required for clarity.
Sometimes I feel like a Chinese painter
who can capture the wind in long grass
with a single, perfect brushstroke.

— *Thanksgiving, 2023*

OWNING A BLACK CAT
ON FRIDAY THE THIRTEENTH

When I switch on the light,
she stirs on the black vinyl chair
where she's been curled asleep,
a darkness disengaging itself
from a greater darkness,
and lands on the hardwood floor
with a ladylike thud. Padding
softly over to where I sit at my desk,
she nuzzles my hand in greeting,
her black nose cold against my skin,
her golden eyes shining a deep
animal affection. It's Friday,
the thirteenth of January, 2023,
and the third week of steady rain.
I am the luckiest man on earth.

IN MEMORY OF A. R. B., 1961–1996

"It could be colder just now, but it isn't."
—*Rick Barot*

The hardest elegy to undertake
is the one for the love you recall
even though it never happened—
the quagmire of clumsy, misshapen
feelings belonging to someone
ages ago who both is, and isn't, you—
who, when they were young,
wounded the girl he wanted,
more than anything else, to win.

This evening, half a century later,
on a winter night without stars,
beneath the censure of the moon,
the mercury's curling into itself
as though tightening into a deep,
insensate sleep. She died at the very
summit of womanhood, for reasons
no research could discover. And now
there's nobody left to apologize to.

THE BIRD FLU

Ordinarily, I prefer
bantam eggs for breakfast,
having convinced myself
they taste better,
and loving in any case
how the soft brown curve of the shell
catches the sunlight
like the rim of the earth
emerging from darkness at dawn
as constellations of cities
extinguish their lights
in imitation of the stars.

But for two weeks now
there've been no eggs of any color
on grocery shelves
anywhere in the Bay Area.
At first I blamed the recent rain,
picturing flooding in Petaluma,
submerged chicken coops,
great rafts of matted feathers
clogging ditches and creeks.
Then today I read about the bird flu,
something I'd never even considered,
and it all turns ominous.

In light of the recent pandemic,
the air seems heavy with portents:
even so simple a thing
as a shortage of eggs
demonstrates how fragile
the natural world is,

and how, in this age
when we can pinpoint our position
to within a few yards
anywhere on the planet,
we seem to have lost
all sense of where we are.

SUMMER ROSES BLOOMING
IN NOVEMBER

In my early teens,
I was for a few years
enthralled with Science Fiction,
an interest that faded in high school
when I discovered poetry.
Now, halfway through
my seventh decade,
I again find myself drawn to it,
as portents of the dystopian future
assert themselves all around me—
from summer roses blooming in November
to rumors of a rising regime
even Orwell wouldn't believe,
that denies the truth of evolution
and scoffs at the light returning
from mirrors placed on the moon.

MANY DEAD MAY BE GATHERED

i.m.: Richard Michael "Mike" Rhodes, 1958-2023

For almost four days now,
I've been dreading the call
that has finally come,
telling me an old friend
who lay near death
has passed away.

During all this time,
it has been bitterly cold—
the wet coastal cold
that reminds us
even in this snowless climate
winter takes dominion
over the final weeks of autumn,
driving birds and small animals
to seek shelter where they may.

Abruptly I remember
that, in the ghost stories
I loved when I was a child,
the temperature plummets
whenever a specter enters.

If that's true, then many dead
may be gathered here unseen,
welcoming into fellowship
the gentle one who early this morning
quietly slipped from the visible world.

They leave no more

trace of their presence
than do the air currents
signing their names
in the registry of dust.

OBLIVION KEEPS ITS DISTANCE

Not long after midnight,
I wake as I so often do,
with the unshakable sense
that both the world and my life
are teetering on the brink of ruin,
although the darkness is eerily still.

Death is of course a whole day
nearer now, but it occurs to me
that such has always been the case,
and for the moment at least,
like a suitor too shy to declare itself,
oblivion keeps its distance.

If I were to go to the window,
raise the blinds, and peer skyward,
I'd still be unable to see the stars.
The moon is the one that drowned Li Bai
the night that he tried to embrace
its reflection in the Yangtze River.

CYPRESSES AND SEPULCHERS

Decades ago, I lived for nearly a year
in a house on the edge of a cemetery,
a silent city of cypresses and sepulchers
where the manicured grass lay in shadow
on even the coldest, brightest days.
The place was watched over by angels
with folded hands and mossy wings,
who never looked up from their prayers
as I walked past them in the purple twilight
heading for somewhere called the future,
the sound of my footsteps deadened
by a most insistent silence, a stillness
that only seemed to deepen as night fell.

STATIC

This morning, unexpectedly,
sunlight coats everything
with a calm, wet brightness,
like the shellac they used to use
to commit the voices of Ella,
Satch, or Billie Holiday to disk—
recordings from which time
and heavy use have long since
worn away the high notes,
leaving only valleys where static
crackles like summer lightning
on a sweltering night in July.

DOING THE DISHES

On the anniversary of my wife Pat's death

Today your passing is a blue glass bowl
in the kitchen sink, the weak light
filling it like a starless, inverted sky.

Or it's some other unremarkable object,
a blunted knife or spoon, one of those things
I never notice, but which endures my touch.

These artifacts have worn your absence
so smooth and shiny it's become a *presence*—
however hard I scrub, they won't come clean.

THE LACK OF YOU

*". . .for wholeness to come like sleep,
or like waking. . ."*
                    —*Deborah Bachels Schmidt*

In the now more than eighteen years
since your passing, it occurs to me
that I have only rarely dreamed of you.

But I carry your absence into my waking
like a stone I swallowed long ago,
or a seed whose tendrils choke my heart.

Your name denotes nobility, and no one
would deny your unassuming dignity,
but I remember your abundant kindness.

Dear Pat, the lack of you sheds its radiance
on even simple things, enfolding my world,
for all its solitude, in effervescent wonder.

THE DISCONSOLATE LIBRARY

Your name, inscribed
in the Book of Errors,
is misspelled.

In its thousands of pages,
the Book of Solitude
is said to contain
only a single word.
Nobody knows
what it is.

The Book of Regret
is so dog-eared
that the pages
have become
as soft as old cloth.
Most of the entries
are blurred by tears.

The Book of Love
is rarely opened,
and then, only
by the foolish.
Before you ask—
we can't be sure
who wrote it.

All words eventually
come home to roost
in the Book of Death,
like a murder of crows
on a black winter branch.

THIS LATE IN THE SEASON

It is a guestbook
that sooner or later
we each must sign.

THE PATIENCE OF PERENNIALS

"The roses don't know why they bloom."
                              —Lee Herrick

Out in the parking lot, in late March,
bedraggled roses shrug off the cold,
having nearly outlasted another winter,
their withered petals edged with rust.

Nothing ever dies completely here
in this half-hearted climate that makes
timid feints at four distinct seasons,
but in the end, knows only wind or wet.

Someday, I suppose, my life will end
quietly in this room, where silent spiders
weave their silken lairs among books,
on a day that doubtless threatens rain.

The roses will neither note nor mark
my passing, consumed as they are
with the patience of perennials,
by the vagabondage of bees.

DAWN UNHOOKS THE STARS

One by one, deliberately,
dawn unhooks the stars
from night's black flannel curtain,
stowing them away at sunrise
in the soft gauze of morning fog,
like the blown glass ornaments
we remember from childhood,
which, when dropped, shattered
into a hundred treacherous shards,
though we were too young then
to realize it was—at least in part—
their latent potential for danger
that had made them beautiful.

THE LAST
OF THE SUMMER LIGHTNING

"I am the shade trees growing near graves cast."
—*Franz Wright, 1953–2015*

You were kinder to me
than you had any reason to be,
replying to my letters,
making brief, brilliant edits
to the few poems
I plucked up the courage to send.

We were acquaintances,
not really friends; to be honest,
I found you somewhat sinister,
for all of my admiration:
a grim and nearly silent ghost
lingering for several years
on the fringes of my circle,
like a chimera barely visible
in the corner of my eye.

It's autumn now in Oberlin—
I imagine the trees along North Professor,
where we both liked to go walking,
are already starting to turn.
The last of the summer lightning
still crackles above the fields
on the outskirts of town.

By now the birds are gone;
but if we were there today,
you wouldn't miss their songs,

teaching me instead
to listen more attentively
to the silence of their absence.

THE PREACHER TURNS HIS BACK ON THE DROUGHT

"Remember my affliction and my wandering..."
—*Lamentations 3:19*

He was a stranger from some farm town,
run out on a rail when months of prayers
and candlelight vigils failed to make
the parched sky yield even a single drop.

In the only surviving photo, his eyes
are slightly wild, brimming with light
from something other than the Lord.
Behind him, the thin horizon, treeless,

tightens to nothingness. There's a date,
handwritten, on the back: *1935*, nothing else.
We're left with an enigma, a Dust Bowl martyr
bereft of a name, a wanderer who clutches

in gnarled hands a forked hickory
divining rod—a dispossessed Moses
with neither flock nor promised land,
following the smell of rain.

AT DUSK IN A NAMELESS CITY

i.m.: Charles Simic, 1938–2023

At dusk in a nameless city,
Shopkeepers are pulling down
The grilles over the display windows
And locking up for the night.

In a deserted dressmaker's shop
On a particularly forlorn corner,
The last rays of the setting sun
Turn all the mannequins crimson.

The madman on the next block
Is really a philosopher in exile.
Hookers in stilettos and ratty furs
Exhale slowly, cigarettes aglow.

No one else is out at this hour,
Save for a woman balancing a bag
Of birdseed, hurrying home to feed
A canary that sings arias from Tosca.

Someone is dead. Someone who loved
This whole flawed, crazy world is dead.
As silence deepens and it grows cold,
All the stars keep their eyes downcast.

NOVEMBER 1900

By the end of the nineteenth century,
men had already invented
iron-clad warships,
a primitive gatling gun,
a rudimentary submarine.
Powered flight was only
three years away,
and the atom bomb,
which would leave a bowl of beautiful
sea-green glass in the desert sand,
fewer than fifty.
My grandmother was born
on a cold morning
in November 1900,
in the final weeks
of Queen Victoria's reign.
Filtered through the smoke
of the Industrial Revolution,
the light that fell on dreaming cities
deepened to sepia.

MAKE A WISH

After reading Yannis Rítsos

The sleepless dead in their enameled boxes
long for caskets of plain, unvarnished pine,
which the roots of trees will eagerly unwrap
like the fingers of children opening presents—
the stars at dawn so many twisted candles,
blown out deliberately, one by one.

PART TWO

You May Begin

FINAL KISS

The gas jets bloom
like thin blue flowers
in the crematorium furnace,
which I've never actually seen
even in my nightmares.

But last night on television
I watched a murder mystery
in which a devious mortician
disposed of his victim's body
by incinerating it until only
a fine white ash remained.

You must have had,
I suppose, a flimsy
cardboard casket,
never meant to last.

I imagine your features,
igniting, retained to the end
that look of preternatural calm
they had when I knelt beside you
in the sanitized light of the morgue
to kiss the icy stillness of your cheek.

How different that final kiss was
from the one I gave you on the chancel
before the congregation on our wedding day.

Love, claimed a poet I knew,
is of all things least illusory.
And even after almost twenty years

I feel your love upholding me
as another wet spring
struggles into blossom,
new leaves like moist green flames
providing a gentler counterpoint
to the awful profusion of fire.

YOU MAY BEGIN

This is not the kind of place
you pictured as the testing room—
open air, menacing clouds, circling birds.

But as you can see, on this vast,
arid plain, among the broken boulders,
sits a single desk, stolen from memory.

Upon it, the examination booklet,
still sealed, awaits you, with a supply
of sharpened pencils smelling of sawdust.

Should you need to use the restroom,
you must first inform the proctor,
which may be difficult, since there's
no one else anywhere in sight.

For that matter, there are no restrooms either.

When you break the seal, don't be surprised
by the rumble of approaching thunder;
don't be surprised if all the pages are blank.

The rising wind whispers in your ear
that, had you reviewed more carefully,
it still would not have helped.

You will have eighty years,
give or take,
to complete the exam.

You may begin.

READING BY NATURAL LIGHT

These days I prefer
to read by natural light,
or, when twilight arrives,
by the soft glow of beeswax
smelling discreetly of honey.
The pale pages, turning
in the stillness, seem kinder
in the daylight, especially
on days when the morning mist
never entirely lifts from the hills
that seem to hang suspended
like dark stars adrift in the fog.

ONE OF THESE MORNINGS

One of these mornings,
perhaps I *will* rise up—
strapping on wings
much the worse for wear:
missing feathers, bent,
stiffened with long disuse.

My song will be a blues
in a minor key, the words
unflinching in their honesty,
but not bereft of comfort.

The solid sky above,
gray as a gravestone,
may well open, but not
to admit my ascent;
I will leave this world,
when I am finally ready,
at the tail end of autumn,
on a day opaque with rain.

THE DAY OF
MICHAEL JACKSON'S FUNERAL

Tuesday, July 7, 2009

The summer the pop singer died,
I was working as a paraeducator
at Thurgood Marshall High School
in the Bayview District, two long
bus rides from where I used to live
in a dilapidated two-room apartment
on the edge of the Tenderloin.
It's hard to believe that was almost
fifteen years ago, a dog's age.
Of the classes in which I assisted,
I can call to mind next to nothing.
We read a novel about black soldiers
in Vietnam, another set in Mexico.
On the day of Michael Jackson's funeral,
the morning fog was late in lifting,
swirling about the classroom windows
like a palimpsest briefly disclosing
traces of smeared illegible type.
Some of the kids begged to be allowed
to watch the singer's burial on an old TV
set up in an adjoining room. *History,*
they pleaded, with an interest in the subject
none of them had ever shown before,
this is history, something to remember.

WITNESS

"To be made whole
by being not just a witness,
but witnessed."

—Ada Limón

In the solitude of these past few years,
my only constant and reliable companions
have been the trees beyond my window:
the Chinese elms whose fissured trunks
make them look as old as the Earth itself,
and the relatively rare Japanese maples
whose searing red, vivid against the green,
burns like the biblical bush,
neither consuming nor consumed.
No God summons me from its moist flames.

If to be made whole is to be witnessed,
then perhaps I was never really here at all,
for I am wounded and seldom leave this room,
confined by the growing fragility of my bones.
The birds I can hear on rare clear days
call, not to me, but to one another,
and the frog-throated foghorns, moaning
like ghosts in the white oblivion of night,
cry to nothing and no one I could name.
I am a little more invisible each day.

I do not dream of being a tree in leaf,
breaking into the pale spring of flesh;
I do not covet the sagacity of crows.
Let me be, if only for one day more,
not only the observer but *observed,*

having perhaps outstayed my welcome
in this world, but by my tenacity
effecting subtle changes I can't know—
my presence merely a smudge
on the face of the Full Snow Moon.

—50—

LABOR DAY WEEKEND, 2022

After two years of discreet absence
fostered by fears of an airborne virus,
the backyard barbeques begin again
to glow across the gray lawns of suburbia
like grim black flowers with burning seeds;
here on the fringes of a great city, wind
works the scrub pines like a pickpocket,
while meat for the sacrifice fattens the air.

GRIEF COUNSELING FOR CATS

There are wonders made conspicuous
only by their absence from this world:

Spaces that mean more by emptiness
than all that might consent to fill them.

Stately black girls with feather boas
the generous color of molten gold.

Window-box poppies eavesdropping
on grief-counseling sessions for cats.

The madrigals clouds sing at dawn
in praise of a flawless lapis lazuli sky.

The orisons of the departed, made,
strangely enough, entirely of praise.

A sparrow with Wallace Stevens's
lost wedding ring glinting in its beak.

The burnished mirror of midnight
where the future stares at the past.

The haloes of countless unuttered
angels breaking abruptly into leaf.

PENANCE

The old woman
with dust in her hair
who accosted me
at the Wimpy Bar
that summer in Cambridge
over forty years ago,
who loudly insisted on
helping me with my tray
because she needed
to *do a penance* for me,
has undoubtedly been
dead for decades now,
and so also perhaps
is the young priest
who was the object
of her illicit desire—
Stuart, *that* was his name—
a "fine, strong man"
whose vestments,
she insisted, glowed
like a vision in the shattered
light of the rose window.

ROBERT JOHNSON

On evenings like this,
the laden air crackles
with the promise of storms.
Drawing the blinds at dusk,
it's possible to imagine,
before I switch on the light,
that my tiny studio apartment
in present-day San Francisco
is filled with smoky voices,
that I'm in a juke joint
near Greenwood, Mississippi,
in the late nineteen thirties.
Perhaps it's the one where even now,
between sets on the makeshift stage,
Robert Johnson is raising a bottle
of poisoned whiskey to his lips.
I want to call to him across the years,
mouthing a warning or a silent plea,
but he's already drifting out of reach.
According to legend, Robert died
on his knees, baying like a dog.
Some claim that this is proof
he had a hellhound on his trail,
while others see only the terminal
stages of strychnine poisoning.

AUTISM BY PROXY

My late father, I realize in hindsight,
must undoubtedly have been
on the autism scale, back in the days
when no one spoke about such things.

Dad was a good father, but stubborn:
a recognized authority on the habitats
of fish populations in New York State,
dead wrong about everything else.

Although I know it was unintentional,
he trained me from a very early age
to distrust innate emotional instincts
it's clear I should never have ignored.

He was adamant that most people
always said exactly what they meant
and should be trusted. Even at seven,
I knew from experience this wasn't so.

Today, I'm afraid, I display symptoms
of mild autism, although I'm fairly sure
that I'm not actually on the spectrum—
I've acquired a sort of autism by proxy.

Still, there are times when I'm unswayed
by my father's explicitly stated assertion
that emotions aren't real and simply vanish
if you resolve to pay them no heed.

THEIRS IS THE MUSIC

In the sixty-seventh year of my age,
as time scrawls its grim predictions
in the slow ache overtaking my bones,
I sit out another dreary coastal spring
as birdsong drips from trees still wet
with the recollection of last night's rain.

Wary of one another, ravens and crows
negotiate their tiny portions of the sky.
Theirs is the music that awakens me
every morning before dawn, the chorus
to which I rise and make my way through
the world, for a few more years at least.

AT FOUR IN THE MORNING

In the country of the ceiling,
the night shadows
are packing to leave.

Sometimes I swear I can almost hear
spiders doing their tightrope walk
on threads the color of moonlight.

WHEN THE LAST PIGEON DIES

I remember reading years ago
that birds are the sole surviving
branch of the dinosaurs;
with a little imagination,
I can almost discern the snout
of a triceratops in the rounded
curve of a pigeon's beak.

Out here in the Sunset
I seldom see pigeons anymore,
only the ubiquitous crows
and ravens whose black attire
makes them look grimly judicial,
as though gathered on their wires
they sit in judgment on us all.

But when I used to live downtown,
I met every morning at the bus stop
a dapper elderly Latino man
on his way to the early Mass,
who was adamant that pigeons
were fallen doves whose shining
white wings had been stained
by untold centuries of sin.

Those birds grow rarer every year.
The day the last pigeon dies,
the old man insisted,
is the day the world will end.

DARKNESS COULD TAKE ME

"Sleep and darkness have a way with pain."
—Taylor Mali

Half asleep before my morning tea,
I feel my body silently refusing
engagement with the daylight.

Were I to close my eyes
even for an instant, I'd see
remnants of my dreams—
posters drained of color,
clinging to a wall abused
by decades of weather.

Darkness could take me then,
and I guess I would let it—
the way a yellow leaf
fallen on a shadowy river
surrenders to the current,
bearing a last scrap of brightness
into the yawning maw of night.

BLUNTED SCISSORS

"At some point, we all disappear."
—*Jennifer Martelli*

At this stage of my life,
I am busily perfecting
the spectacular finale,
my disappearing act.

I have begun to observe
even the most ordinary object,
a blunted pair of scissors, say,
as if from an immense distance.

And even though it rests
plainly on the desk before me,
the shrunken shadow it casts
is long since consigned to memory.

RADIANCE

> *"...how meticulously*
> *Renaissance painters rendered light."*
> — Cyrus Cassells

Fleeing the torpor of Madrid,
I sought the darkness of the Prado,
weary from lugging my backpack
through white streets where doves
rose in a flurry of wingbeats
from elegant fountains.

Centuries before the camera,
the Old Masters layered oil so thin
it achieved actual translucence
onto boards of fragrant cedar
from forests already vanishing
almost a thousand years before.

Most of all I loved Caravaggio
and the Frères La Tour, who were
as concerned with what lay hidden
in the shadows as with what yielded
to the insistence of candlelight
or the pallor of the moon.

I had turned twenty a month before
in the Bay of Naples, the solstice
gifting me a sunburn so fierce
my skin peeled like parchment,
leaving me alone in a hostel bunk
fighting a raging fever and chills.

In the city beyond the galleries,
engulfed in fumes and roaring traffic,
the rest of my life awaited me,
both beguiling and baffling, bathed
in radiance that spilled from the sky
with the authority of an annunciation.

A WALK WITH MARY OLIVER

"But holiness is visible, entirely."
—Mary Oliver, 1935–2019

It matters very little
that we never met,
even less that she's
been dead for several years.
Knowing the value of silence,
she would not choose to speak
even if she were still able to.
Instead we would stroll together
along the edge of a pond at dusk—
her presence rapt, if invisible—
listening intently as crickets
shrilled and bullfrogs groaned.
She, who handled language
as though it were light,
yet felt the weight of clouds,
must have sussed out there were
limits to poetry, that it dare not
compete with a screech owl
scrawling its beautiful shadow
on the page of the rising moon.

WAKING

Unwrap the morning slowly,
the stillness, shadows, and dust.
Step gently from bedclothes
as from a winding sheet—
or that other sheet, a sail,
already veering off course.
When you emerge, blinking,
into radiance, you will still
remember, for only a moment,
the smoldering ruins of dreams
bombed almost into oblivion
in the occupied country of sleep.

SOLITARY CONFINEMENT

"Some rooms are like cages."
—Paul Simon

This apartment is pleasant enough,
with its stacks of dog-eared books,
its fly-specked Irish flag on one wall,
sagging beneath the unshorn dust.

On clear mornings, my window
admits a radiance ruling the floor
through incompletely drawn blinds
in long, rigid bars of molten light.

Yet after years spent mostly indoors,
this space begins to seem like a prison
for the more stringent cage of my body—
dirty plaster abutting barricades of bone.

There are spiders secreted in the silence,
tightrope-walking the silken lace of hunger;
somewhere, apparently, there are birds.
But who gives a damn about birds?

SMALL-MOUTHED BASS

When I finally reeled it in,
the cruel hook protruding
from its pierced upper lip,
it flopped for a moment
against the wooden planks
in the bottom of the boat—
gills like flightless wings
feathered black with blood—
and then lay quiet. Barely
seven, I'd caught it myself,
albeit with help from Daddy;
I'd made my first kill. Later,
as it sat white and naked
on my plate, steaming flesh
flaking from the tines of my fork,
I could have sworn I could
actually taste its breathless
stillness, the nagging guilt
caught in my throat
like a tiny bone.

A KIND OF FRAGILE MUSIC

Murio's Trophy Room on Haight Street

For the moment at least,
the ancient analog clock
keeps not even tavern time.
There are no other patrons.
The clink of glass on glass
as the bored bartender
arranges mugs on a shelf
produces a kind of fragile music
amplified by the row of empty stools,
the muteness of the darkened jukebox,
the green-felt reticence of the pool table.

THIS LATE IN THE SEASON

"There is the question of how to love.
—January Gill O'Neil

As incredible as it seems to me,
it's been nearly eighteen years
since your death. In this rainy
place where it never snows,
I remember the white helmet
of plaster and bandages
capping your skull like a crust
no step would break, your face,
cold and remote beneath it,
like a patch of black ice:
a peril whose rigid beauty
both compels and frightens.
It was deep winter then;
now another nameless
year is sliding into autumn,
whose gilded edges even here
put a brave face on loss.
There is the question of how
to love, how best to spend
whatever time remains.
This skittish weather
provides no answers,
as jays fuss and squabble
in trees still green with rage
even this late in the season.

FOR A BLACK UNICORN

i.m.: Audre Lorde, 1934–1992

Discovering your work
at Oberlin, decades ago,
I was instantly taken
by its forthright fervor,
keen eye for telling detail,
and unflinching opposition
to every entrenched injustice,
however blatant or subtle.
You were black and lesbian,
but never exclusively so—
your art a refining fire
illuminating a maelstrom
where, from the crucible
of human suffering,
flames of outrage arose
on incandescent wings.

JUST POSSIBLY. . .

. . .Anton Nyquil,
a seventeenth-century
Flemish pharmacist,
invented the cold remedy
that still bears his name,
while the twist-off bottle cap
was actually the brainchild
of one Israel "Ira" Twistoff,
a Russian Jewish immigrant
who patented it in Brooklyn
in the early months of 1920,
around the same time that,
in Zurich, a station agent
named Hansel Addfare
initiated a ticketing system
allowing commuters to board
trains much more efficiently—
clutching their briefcases,
their green felt homburgs
and their sandwich bags
courtesy of an obscure
Serbian grocery clerk
known as Goran Ziploć.

NEW HAMPSHIRE

For Janet Wildung

The leaves in New Hampshire
will have turned golden by now,
obedient to the chill in the air.

What birds remain as summer's light
bronzes into autumn, what songs
they stumble through, I've forgotten.

I have been absent for far too long.
Along the rocky coast, the water
turns topaz, shouldering the wind.

BEFORE DAYBREAK

i.m.: Patricia Lewis Smith, 1953–2005

That you were cremated
means that, for the past
nearly eighteen years,
there's been no grave to visit,
no place to locate
an absence that seems
to spread like ashes
across a wounded sky
in the birdless silence
an hour before daybreak.

Indeed, on this first day
of autumn, the lack of you
is apparent everywhere:
in the topmost branches,
as the first light illuminates
a few always-green leaves
borne aloft like prayers
above the lower darkness,
in the sounds of sunrise
turning over in its sleep.

In the end, I am only
what love has left me.
I don't look for reunions
in some kingdom beyond
the sky, vague supernatural
promises empty of comfort.
But it is true that sometimes,
as dawn takes shape around me,

it's possible to believe once more
in your vast, human tenderness.

OFFERING WINGS

"Everything about the house seemed alien to me."
—James Tate 1943–2015

I've been staring at these four walls
for so long now I no longer see them:
shelves, books, photographs dissolve,
and I abruptly find myself standing
alone and naked in the yard where
I've been unable to venture for years.

Although the trees here are green
throughout the year, the wind blows
a few orphaned leaves, brown and dry,
through the withered grass at my feet.
If the morning is cold, I cannot feel it;
sunlight spills easily through my body.

Everything about the room I've eluded
seems alien to me, a forsaken country
to which I am sure I shall never return.
My translucent heart is a fist of blood
clenching and unclenching in my ribs.
Circling crows seem to be offering wings.

AFTER I'M GONE

Whether there's a Heaven or not,
after I'm gone I'll be reunited
with my late wife, if only as dust

drifting out to sea at dawn
as the city that was our home
wakes into radiance below.

What will be left but music?
The wind will moan a lament
like the old country blues I love,

while the setting moon
shines like the resonator
of a National guitar.

THE FAILING LIGHT

This late in the day,
the failing light evokes
the sheen I've often noticed
in the chill before dawn—
a thin gold foil
gilding the leaves
until they resemble
the elaborate molding
on antique ceilings
that recalls no foliage
in Heaven or on Earth.

All the birds, at this hour,
have fallen silent. The bells
of St. Anne of the Sunset,
hollow and hesitant,
seem to be tolling
in the distant past.

When the first cold stars pierce
the bronze breastplate of the sky,
and I am about to draw the blinds,
all that is real is that metallic glow
withdrawing with sure and silent steps
across the ruins of the winter lawn.

OLD GRAVEYARD

Not infrequently,
I dream of an old graveyard
after heavy snow—
headstones covered
like abandoned furniture
whose hunched shapes
I can't quite make out
beneath drop cloths
in a house long vacant.
The only tenants now
are the sun that burns
coldly for all its ferocity,
and a few vagrant leaves,
withered and fragile,
that write their names
on the stony pages
where once were epitaphs.

PART THREE

*Extravagant Beauty
Everywhere*

SMELLING FAINTLY
OF DAMPENED EARTH

"The Bible will rest on the back of a griffin."
—Nancy Willard, 1936–2017

I have observed the intricate teak
lecterns in the bellies of old churches,

the ponderous hidebound Testaments
they are forced to bear. I have longed

to run my fingers over heavy pages
smelling faintly of dampened earth.

Brightly colored saints whose wings
are feathered only with feeble light

promise no salvation I would choose;
grant me instead the lamp of language—

on the carvèd shoulders of the beast,
metaphor trembles, poised to soar.

STATIONS

I didn't grow up steeped in the folklore
from which Vasko Popa would fashion
tales of wolves and candles set adrift
down Slavic rivers seeking other worlds.
But I did inherit, on my mother's side,
the nutbrown buckeyes of northern Ohio,
impenetrable as varnished hardwood,
the light these weird seeds always wore
like the sheen of recent rain.
And I remember being shown,
once or twice, houses—
on the now disused byways
of the nineteenth century—
brooding over some remote crossroads,
windows dulled as if by ancient pain—
places I was told had formerly been
stations on the Underground Railroad
sheltering fugitive slaves bound for Canada.
The mere presence of these unassuming
wooden dwellings scarred by bitter weather
hinted that even the flatness of the lake plain,
with its fields, silos, and nondescript trees,
might once have had a history.

FOR THE ANNIVERSARY
OF MY ARRIVAL

October 6, 1987

Thirty-five years ago today,
I boarded a 737 in Newark
with a single suitcase,
a copy of *Answered Prayers,*
and a sandwich in my carry on,
an uncertain future ahead.

I changed planes in Minneapolis,
seeing only a crowded concourse
where I have never been since.
The in-flight movie on the way
to San Francisco was a silly
comedy involving Bigfoot.

The stars were already out
when I landed, the moist,
hot air evoking an East Coast
August rather than early autumn,
the night sky chafed by the glow
of the city a few miles to the north.

This was when it all began.
I couldn't know then that I would grow
old here, find love only to lose it,
become accustomed to the decay
that haunts the Pacific, like an old tune
so stuck in your head you've stopped listening.

WILLOW ROCHE

When my father hired Willow Roche
to drive us up the Irish coast,
the old man insisted on sealing the deal
with a dram or two down at his local,
while my mother, sister, and I sat
waiting in his car in the parking lot,
Mom fretting more and more
the longer they remained inside.

When they emerged, the whiskey
stench hung heavy about them,
and, in Willow's decrepit little Mini,
on that hot July half a century ago,
the fumes made me dizzy, as if
for a moment I were an outsider
from some more sanguine place,
surveying the scene from above.

As we wove in and out of our lane,
Old Willow, gracious and garrulous,
boasted that his name was known
to any man in Ireland's thirty-two.
Temporarily unmoored from the flesh,
my timorous spirit quivered between
his weathered brogue and the sheer
drop to my left, where the bright tide
gnawed the boulders at a distance.

MORE AWARE OF BIRDS

There's no need
to revisit the dust
swirling in galaxies
through the brown air
of a room with blinds
partially drawn even at noon.
Suffice to say that, in my sixties,
I've grown more aware of birds—
their cold, inhuman cries,
their unsettling beauty,
the rush of air beneath
wings lifting into twilight,
the hard, reptilian glitter
in their eyes, should one
dare stray close enough
to where I sit at my window
that, for an instant, I meet
and almost condone
that fathomless cruelty.

FASHIONED OF PURE LIGHT

Old spiderwebs glow faintly in dim corners,
abandoned highways fashioned of pure light.
Where now the being who brooded at the center,
patient and deadly as a minotaur—
who felt the slightest quiver of the strands,
the miniscule footsteps of a fly?

WITH STARTLING CLARITY

Years ago, I walked at dusk
down an unfamiliar street
on the Upper West Side,
past elegant apartment buildings
dating from the 1920s
whose brickwork and elaborate
Arthurian doorways the decades
had dimmed to the dun of soot.

In from Jersey, and out of my depth,
I was looking in vain for the address
of some party I'd been invited to,
and, after so long, I can't remember
whether or not I ever found it.

What I do recall with startling clarity
is passing the open door of a bar
where the jukebox inside was blaring
"Mondo Sinistro," one of my favorite
Al Stewart tunes, something
familiar enough to ground me,
allowing me to get my bearings
as the overcast sky above
darkened into ambient light.

THE LAST
OF THE SUMMER BONFIRES

I wound up here
as almost everybody does,
shedding a past that I'd outgrown,
drawn to the edge of the continent,
letting the dark surf curl at dusk
around my ankles as the sun
sank beneath a watery horizon,
leaving a slash of savage light.

How strange it seems to realize
I thought myself old at thirty,
barely having taken charge of my life—
when I was bent on redefining myself,
and most of what I'd learn of love
still lay ahead, an unexpected miracle
already present in the upswept sparks,
destined to set off sparklers in my bones.

The weeks ahead would gradually gray
as autumn settled in and made its stand,
but when I think of those lonesome nights
when the last of the summer bonfires
crackled on the sand at Ocean Beach,
I picture seagulls pinned like seraphim,
the alabaster arches of their wings
tinged with a febrile Pentecostal fire.

DETAILS AT ELEVEN

Concerning the ubiquity of loss,
there's very little anyone can say.
On winter nights in the last century,
the cobalt glow of monstrous televisions
that still presented life in black and white
embalmed the viewers' faces like wet lead.
Nothing today can touch that solitude.

UNIQUELY AMERICAN

Benjamin Franklin advocated
the adoption of the wild turkey
as our national bird, the creature
uniquely American. The choice
may have been more appropriate
than he knew, since even before
domestic turkeys lost the gift of flight,
becoming so fat their spindly legs
could barely support their weight,
the species was known to be
abysmally stupid. It's rumored,
although I haven't confirmed it,
that whole flocks have been seen
standing outside in a rainstorm
with necks craned upward
and beaks opened wide,
drinking until they drown.

A HOLE IN TWILIGHT'S POCKET

If I lived near a creek,
deer might drift down
to its banks to drink at dusk,
the starless night in their eyes—
not here in a city where the moon
floats on water gathered in gutters
like a coin that has fallen unnoticed
through a hole in twilight's pocket,
a swarming city where autumn skies
are mostly overcast and, in the Presidio,
wind foraging through the eucalyptuses
still weeps for banished redwoods.

IMPONDERABLES

My personal theology
holds that God exists
on the grounds that there's no way
this much could go wrong by itself.

From day to day, I'm not concerned
with big issues such as global warming
or the endless war in Ukraine
but with a flood of unpleasant
coincidences that suggest
there's a force in the universe
that means me harm—
or at the very least,
has a nasty sense of humor.

Living alone, I often find the stillness
oppressive, yet the phone never rings
unless I'm in the shower, the doorbell
shrills through the dusty air
only when I'm on hold
during an important phone call,
the damaged package is always
the one I wanted or needed most.

I'm reminded of the painted saints
I saw many years ago
in the gloom of French cathedrals,
whose bewildered wooden eyes
offered no excuses, even then.

I'm aided in my daily struggle
with these imponderables by my cat,

who pads across the hardwood floor
bent on some errand of her own,
and who, I feel sure,
has no answers either.

SUSTENANCE

"I am aware it is not good to eat oatmeal alone."
—*Galway Kinnell, 1927–2016*

This morning,
against my late teacher's advice,
I ate oatmeal alone.

I am not as troubled by its consistency
as Galway appears to have been.

In it, I taste the countless generations
of Scottish or Irish tenant farmers
whose survival depended
on this plain but wholesome sustenance.

I taste too the patience of the soil,
the way the forsaken furrows in winter
offer up their harvest of stones
to nourish churches, cottages, and barns
as the grain nourishes our bodies.

I do not require, as Galway did,
an imaginary companion
from among the poets of the past
to share this simple meal.
But I keep his place set
should he care to join me.

MY FUTURE SAT WITH ME

I remember birdsong
before dawn,
the rising sun
whitening the windows
of the tenements
across the way
with savage fire.
My future sat with me
in a tiny room
emerging from shadow,
like a crazy uncle
one tolerates
but knows not to trust.
I was twenty-seven.
The years ahead
seemed more threat
than promise.

EXTRAVAGANT BEAUTY EVERYWHERE

The summer I spent in England was,
I realized to my surprise this morning,
exactly forty years ago. I was 25.

Paul McCartney's *Tug of War* was
the number one album in Britain,
"Take it Away" a chart-topping single
that played incessantly on our bus
as we rolled past Stonehenge
in the golden morning mist.

It seemed only fitting
that one of the Beatles
should provide the soundtrack
for our jaunts through the rolling
green English countryside.

I remember formal gardens
at the great house Audley End
where I walked as sunset
gilded the walls and trees
with a lovely young woman
whose name and face
I have long since forgotten.

I remember too a lone seagull
pinned like a crucifix
to the thin sky above quilted fields
many miles from the sea.

What I do not remember
is how it felt to *be* me then—

an interloper beset on all sides
by the scent of dew on new roses,
the follies, the ancient towers—
extravagant beauty everywhere,
and real life still somehow
unimaginably distant,
the future mocking me,
just out of reach.

THE SOLEMNITY OF CLOCKS

I miss the solemnity
of analog clocks,
the way each solitary
tick shatters the silence
like a judge pronouncing
a death sentence, the way
their constant need of winding
reminds us of time's passage,
making us acolytes who serve
what we feel but cannot touch.
Time knows us well but refuses
to pity us, distant as the last
mourner at our deathbed.
And an ancient analog clock
hangs like an astonished moon
in that cold room, every tock
counting down to a final breath.

LET'S SAY

Let's say that you choose
the place where you live,
much as a corpse chooses its casket,
a casket unwittingly chooses its grave.
And let's say your decision extends
beyond your seedy furnished room
into the wider world outside—
the sentient, secretive trees,
the sky with its feather boa of birds.
Let's say that one day, out of nowhere,
you knew that a choice had been made,
although you could not recall making it—
a choice you could never possibly undo.
Would knowing make any difference? *Would* it?

AS THE DARK WITHDRAWS

Deep rivers lie awake in their soft beds,
feeling the weight of starlight on their backs.
Near dawn, the forest creatures come to drink
along their banks, eyes eerie with faint light.
There is no silence as the dark withdraws—
a thousand tiny, furtive scurryings
make muted music in the undergrowth
until the moment when the birds begin.

THE UBIQUITY OF PAIN (PINOCCHIO)

My wooden limbs
were stiff and awkward,
but, with the grace of flesh,
came the first knowledge
of the ubiquity of pain.
One shouldn't have to bargain
to be recognized as real.
Beneath my fine white gloves,
fingers that were twigs,
touching the blood in leather,
go on accusing the axe
of nothing less than murder.

ONE SWELTERING NIGHT IN TEXAS

Outside, the heat climbed in moist rags
from the asphalt, smudging the Winnebagos,
the No Vacancy sign, the ice machine
(out of order), the enormous day moon.

Inside, we'd turned the air conditioner
all the way up as we gathered around
the color TV, both of these things novelties
we didn't have back home in New Jersey.

My sister and I drank grapefruit Tang
from Dixie cups, claiming that much, at least,
in common with the astronauts. *That's
one small step*, barely visible, ghosting gray.

I never told anyone how jealous I was,
at twelve, of those first moonwalkers, knowing
that cerebral palsy, my inturned toes and always
fragile balance, would forever bind me to the Earth.

As night fell, heat still climbed in moist rags
from the asphalt, smudging the Winnebagos,
the No Vacancy sign, the ice machine
(out of order), the distant, mocking moon.

NORTH OF DENVER

North of Denver, the open prairie,
starting from the base of the Rockies,
which rise abruptly, without foothills,
is a drab expanse of faded grass
that, even on clear days, vanishes
into the east, into an indistinct smudge
of yellow that's not exactly a horizon.

What astonishes a visiting city dweller
is the vastness of the sky—an inverted
bowl of deep blue Depression glass
where, high above, a single hawk,
too distant for us to discern clearly,
observes our progress without interest
before veering away and moving on.

INCONSEQUENTIAL THINGS

"When dreams no longer mattered,
when I became too broken to write—"
        —*Johanna Ely*

When dreams no longer mattered,
I began to pay closer attention
to inconsequential things—
the way a dying petal
fallen from a houseplant
left a vivid splash of pink
on the windowsill,
like splatter from an artist's brush
that'd somehow missed the drop cloth.

I began to listen more attentively
even to faint and furtive noises,
and most especially to silence.

I knew without being told
love was now far behind me.

My pen lay mute
on a page unscathed
save for a single stroke
like the one left behind
by a fish that, free of the hook,
expels a ribboning trail of blood
as it descends into the depths.

LIGHT KNOCKS AT THE WINDOW

It's a Monday morning in late April,
in the last days of the republic
and the final years of the world.
No sound comes from the yard
outside, but the sun is shining
and light knocks at the window
with disturbing urgency, evoking
less a passing friend than an agent
of the secret police arriving at dawn
to arrest you for some crime of which
you have always been guilty, though
you've never known quite what it is.

A HIVE OF DISAPPOINTMENT

German Bible, nineteenth century

The embossed leather cover,
long since curled at the corners,
has been darkened by time
and a patient intimacy
with the touch of the dead.

Hands now ages dust,
taking up the heft of it
in the eternal twilight
of a discarded century,
cried dumbly for mercy.

Fingertips stumbled
over chapter and verse,
caressing the hope of Heaven—
the whisper of skin on paper
almost a kind of prayer.

God, here, really is in the details:
The double-columned pages
of ponderous Gothic characters
comprise a hive of disappointment,
swarming before our eyes.

ONE TRIUMPH AND TWO FAILURES

i.m.: Dr. C. Lavett Smith, 1927–2015

Despite my precarious balance
and the way my inturned toes
refuse to remain securely planted
between the rocks where they
might find purchase, I manage
to climb the nearly vertical trail
up the Palisades to the top,
my ascent darkened by my father's
steadier shadow covering me,
his sure-footedness accusing
my awkwardness. Only once
am I tempted to turn my head
to survey the distance we've come.
"Don't," Dad says quietly but firmly,
an unfamiliar note of panic
in his voice. "Don't look."

It's many years later. The day
after my wife's memorial service,
Dad calls to read me the riot act,
having heard that I went out to eat
with friends upon leaving the sanctuary.
"It's cheaper to eat at home," he scolds,
totally unaware that there's an emotional
component to any of this. At that moment,
I want, for reasons impossible to explain,
to be able to love him. I cannot.

Ten years farther on, Dad passes away
in a hospice in Colorado. His memories,

and his cruelties, have preceded him in death.
When Mom calls with the news, I feel,
even at sea level in San Francisco,
a precipice, a sheer drop at my back.
There is to be no funeral, so I remain at home.
He's one more person among so many
that I have failed to save.

VALENTINE'S DAY, 2020

i.m.: Patricia Lewis Smith, 1953—2005

At daybreak this morning, deep
into the fifteenth year of your death,
I noticed a long-bodied cellar spider
dangling in a corner of the room
on a thread so thin it was invisible—
the dark teardrop of its body suspended,
motionless, above an emptiness
that might give way at any moment.

THREE SIGNS THAT YOU ARE BOTH A POET AND A CAT OWNER

1.
While you are reading aloud
a poem you're revising,
the cat yawns,
and you discard the draft.

2.
You own six different editions
of *Old Possum's Book of Practical Cats,*
not counting those included
in your multiple copies
of Eliot's *Collected Poems.*

3.
When filling out a questionnaire
prior to visiting the vet,
you are asked what brand
of dry food you feed your cat,
and without stopping to think,
you respond, IAMBS.

I WANT TO BE LAURELED IN OBLIVION

I don't aspire to the celebrity
accorded Frost or Ginsberg,
to the visionary lyrical intensity
of Bob Dylan or Dylan Thomas.
Let my poems be remembered,
when they are remembered at all,
as well-crafted if not well known,
as an authentic and honest voice
stubbornly sounding in nihility,
proclaiming that the most praised
is seldom, if ever, akin to the best.
I want to be as solid as Paul Siebel,
Rodriguez, or Jackson C. Frank,
their struggles validated by failure,
by exquisite, palpable yearning.
I want to be laureled in oblivion
alongside Audrey Wurdemann,
Edwin Rolfe, and Kenneth Fearing.

IN THE NEXT LIFE

In the next life, I'm waiting for a bus
somewhere in suburban New Jersey.

It's a warm spring evening
as the last of the sunset fades,
the moment when the first stars
begin to appear, holes nibbled
in the coarse cloth of the sky.

The leaves beneath the streetlight,
stirring in a barely noticeable breeze,
glow like soft green wings
poised on the brink of flight.

They are the only angels
I will ever need.

ALL THE FRENZIED CITY AT THEIR FEET

"Lasciate ogne speranza, voi ch'intrate."
—*Inferno, Canto III*

Dante and Virgil, on a modern street—
seen just as they're depicted by Doré—
have all the frenzied city at their feet,

but are appalled before the senseless fray.
No shades encountered in the depths of Hell
have terrified the pair in quite this way.

Never did brimstone leave so foul a smell
as issues from a passing Greyhound bus;
the very air around them seems unwell.

Beset by sins too terrible to discuss,
the poets redescend into the pit;
neither will ever write or speak of us.

JACK AND JILL

After such a long time,
I'd say they've forgotten
the tiring climb to the top,
the well at the summit,
sun sharp on the water.

Now it's all about the descent:
the spinning tangle of grass and sky,
clouds already red with evening,
stars that may be harbingers
of concussion—or simply stars.

I'd say that, at heart, every story
is finally concerned with falling.
It's a long way still to the bottom;
in the village far below, the lights
are slowly starting to come on.

INDEX OF TITLES

ABOUT THE AUTHOR

ROBERT LAVETT SMITH lives in San Francisco. He holds a B.A. in French from Oberlin College, where he also studied creative writing with Stuart Friebert and David Young, and an M.A. in English from the University of New Hampshire, studying with Charles Simic and Mekeel McBride. After graduating from UNH, he joined the Master Class at the 92nd Street YMHA in New York City, where he studied with Galway Kinnell. He has authored four small-press chapbooks and five previous full-length efforts, *Everything Moves with a Disfigured Grace, Smoke In Cold Weather: A Gathering of Sonnets, The Widower Considers Candles, Sturgeon Moon,* and *Collected Early Poems.*

A NOTE ON THE FONTS

This book is set in Requiem, designed by Jonathan Hoefler in 1992. The old-style serif font, inspired by the inscriptional capitals in Ludovico Vicentino degli Arrighi's 1523 writing manual *Il Modo de Temperare le Penne* and by the chancery calligraphy of the period, is one of the most elegant renderings of the classical alphabet. Trajan, the relief font, designed in 1989 by Carol Twombly for Adobe, is based on the Roman square capitals originally etched into the base of Trajan's Column in Rome in the first century.

Printed in the USA
CPSIA information can be obtained
at www.ICGtesting.com
JSHW021138060924
69108JS00001B/6